Crossfires of Spiritual WAR

Memoirs of

Arthur Barcinas

Dedication

This book is dedicated to my mother Alicia Abi Barcinas.
After three years, I realize the poet in you has possessed my soul.
I hope you enjoy it,
Till I see you again…

Table of Contents

This is my life

WARNING

The following book DOES contain graphic content
and may not be suitable for disbelievers
Hater discretion is advised

Sometimes you have to back up to move foward

THE ORANGE ROSE

The Orange Rose is a symbol of beauty
The Orange Rose is unconditional love
The Orange Rose is kind and forgiving
The Orange Rose is our blessing from above
The Orange Rose is a wonderful Mother
The Orange Rose is you

KISS

You knew your time had come
As I gave you one last kiss
A kiss I wish I could forget
A kiss I can't stop reliving
A kiss I still can't accept
A kiss that was our last goodbye

WISH

You used to tell us if that time ever came, pull the plug
Never imagining that moment would come
Well, your wish was granted☹
I wish it was me instead
Now through your wish, I am the vessel your words are said……

REMEDY

Obese heart………

No cure
Still searching for answers, as I reminisce our last moments together….

Three years later……
My soul mending
Stitched slowly by the love of my family
My spirit reviving
Bandaged by the prayers of my people
My mind healing
Writing is my anesthesia

TEARS

My unhappy day…

The day we cherish and love our mothers
I will never forgive myself, not being there for your last
Now that at I look back, it didn't feel right
Wishing you Happy Mother's day 1000 miles away
A baby on the way
No way of knowing these were your last days
Shedding tears as I write this book

Tears of regret
Tears of denial
Tears of anger
Tears of a son, who lost his mother☹

UNDER THE RAINBOW

Somewhere under the rainbow
Feeling blue
The land that I live in is not a lullaby

Somewhere under the rainbow
Skies are grey
And none of my dreams come true

Somedays I wish there were no stars
As I wake up to cloudy days in front of me
Where trouble melts like lemon tears
Suffocating from the smoke of the chimney
That's where I'll be

Somewhere under the rainbow
Blue birds cry
Birds cry under the rainbow
I can't stop crying

If sad little blue birds cry under the rainbow
Oh why, oh why, can't I stop crying?

DEAR JESUS

I rise from the depths of hell once again
Unconditionally, you continue to love me
I am not an evil man
Just a man who is weak of the flesh
Guilty, of succumbing to the pleasures of the world
Maybe, this is your way of forcing me to do the right thing
But what is the right thing?
Is it sacrificing everything for you?
Sacrificing everything for my family?
Now that I'm in your hands I will trust you
As you break me down and redesign my heart and soul
Let us pray……………
I pray that whatever you decide as my fate, I accept
I know you see my struggle
I know you see me trying my best to give it all to you
It's not easy
I'm not going to lie
Ridiculed by non-believers and men without faith
Still tempted by Satan
Even more so, as I walk with you
My family sees my evolution
Not only as a man, but a man of God
I hope you see it too

So thank you Jesus,
Thanks and thanks again
I hope I don't let you down
I know if I want to see my mother in heaven

I can't let you down……….

Love,
Art

P.S. Thank you for blessing me with the gift of writing
I love it☺

THE COMEBACK

That's ok, she'll be back
She always comes back….
In my dreams

AFTERMATH

Unchartered territory
Still numb
Baby on the way
Depression
Denial
Guilt
Thinking back
Would of
Should of
Could of
Jesus takes my hand, like cool hand Luke
Family wounded
Stepping up one by one
Baby is here…
A sigh of relief
Easing the grief
I feel like I'm possessed by you……
A different man
A different plan
Every move I make
Every step I take
Thinking, what would she do?
Days getting brighter
Family getting tighter
Your traditions alive
Through your memories I thrive
Still hard, still pain
Trying to be a better man

So much more to gain
Accepting
Dealing
Learning how to cope
As I write this book
For you
About you
Hoping
No, believing
We will be together again......

IS THAT YOU?

Are those your eyes I see in my daughter?
That beautiful dragon fly in disguise?
Or the mysterious butterfly that hovers over my children by the Orange Rose garden?
Is she that curious hummingbird that visits me when I'm feeling blue?

Is that you?

20 YEARS BACK

Blessed, with a family I can't afford
Blessed, with a family that can afford me
Feeling ashamed when I have to ask
Grateful, the Godfather has my back
Thank you Godfather….

As I attempt to take the corporate world by storm
Caught up in a corporate economic storm

My church attacked by the enemy
Biggest enemy is myself

Smoking a pack a day
Working out every day
Can hardly afford to pay attention
Searching for that BIG BREAK in life
Breaking my back
Can't look back
Tough times behind us
Tougher times ahead
No more drinking and drugs
Just a little Kush to the head

I miss my mom every day
I still can't believe she's gone…………

I feel my wife under pressure…………….

Through good times and bad
In sickness or health
Rich or poor
Wishing for more
I can't have her sad
Happy wife
Happy life

A young family, I started late
A forty something
Now husband, Christian and dad, trying to relate

There's no instructions on how to do it right
My writing keeps my mind right
As I write about my pain and struggles I fight, but not alone
There's no I in team
Surrounded by angels
My family
My church
My friends
My dream team

So as time keeps on tripping, slipping, dripping
into my past……
I wish I could fly like an eagle to the sea of redemption

As I pay for the mistakes I made, 20 years back….

THE PROBLEM

He was never accountable
Pointing fingers, searching for the problem
Evading the truth, wouldn't swallow his pride
Always the victim….
He was too concerned, searching for the problem
Delusional, living a lie
Getting high, watching time fly….
While the problem was in his spirit
The problem was in his soul
The problem was in his heart
The problem was in his mind
Consumed, searching for the problem
He was too busy diagnosing the problem
He didn't realize………
He was the problem

IT HURTS

The truth hurts
But lies hurt even more

FOOL

Giant ego
One track mind
Thinking he's cool, like Arthur Fonzarelli
Thinks he's finer than fine wine
Cocky
Conceited
Arturo…….. was a friend of mine

Lived for today
Didn't think of tomorrow
Broke many hearts
Causing pain
Never gave
Always borrowed
Tried to pay back
Breaking his family's back
Loved the women
The women loved him back……..
Center of attention
Life of the party
NOW BATTING, #23, ARTURO BARCINAS
AKA, shallow Arty

Misunderstood
His mother hoping for change
Praying one day he would
Knowing he could

Hitting rock bottom
Not once
Not twice
But three times a lady………
My angel
My heart
I tore her apart
She picked me up
Time and time again
Then all of a sudden
She's gone

PREGAME

My church is being attacked, so am I
God is telling me to get ready for war
I didn't realize being a Christian was so hard

VICTIM

Trapped in his own skin
A sheep in wolfs clothing
Undeniable beauty
No intention of sin……
The women get weak
The men loathe, and some get weak
Blessing or curse?
Judged by those who can't relate

COMFORT ZONE

Comfortable, feeling uncomfortable
They say it's the path to change
But who are they to say?

TO ALL THE GIRLS WHO'VE LOVED ME BEFORE

To all the girls who've loved me before
The one's who let me in their door
I'm glad we shared our hearts
So sad we grew apart
To all the girls who've loved me before

To all the girls who held me tight
And may I say, it was pure delight
For teaching me to grow, I owe a lot I know
To all the girls who've loved me before

To all the girls who cut, like a knife
Thank God you're someone else's wife
I'm glad we grew apart
From the bottom of my heart
To all the girls who've loved me before

To all the girls who shared my bed
The ones I won't ever forget
Who I adore the most
I'd like to make a toast
To all the girls who've loved me before

The summer winds came blowing in
Every time I tried to stay…
The summer winds came blowing in
And carried me away

PRICELESS

Enthusiast to her taste
Captivated by her touch
Infatuated with her soul
23 shades of Arturo
As I worship her from head to toe
Feign for her lips
Enticed by her creamy thighs
Craving her pheromones like, mothers milk
My spirit adrenalized by her soft, unblemished derrière, as it glistens off the moonlight like the shooting star of seduction
Invited, by the arch in her back
My senses flustered by her narcotic scent
And then….
Slowly….
Willingly….
She peels off her G
A sight for the sorest eyes
LEGIT….
Hypnotized, as she shakes her ass to that sexy little dance
Mesmerized, while she looks back at me like Aphrodite
The goddess of love…
To my ultimate delight, she whispers in my ear
Take me from behind………..
Stimulated by the aroma that fills the air with her intoxicating euphoria
Family jewels shining bright

My mind doing summersaults of love
Thinking to myself
Damn it feels good to be me…
Ridiculed by her tightness
Titillated toes like Fred Astaire
Our bodies dance in pure glee
Perfect beat
Impeccable rhythm…
Like Mozart and the sexual symphony
Bedazzled by each thrust
Prolonging every stroke, like it's the last
Possessed, in a state of cosmic, galactic, orgasmic bliss..........

No words can describe
Priceless….

WAKE UP CALL

It wasn't till I wrote about it
I realized, how fucked up it was

CARTWHEELS

It seems the enemy likes to attack on Thursday.
The last month of Fridays have been days of recuperation,
as I find myself doing cartwheels in hell, attempting to save
my family…….

Lord, please give me strength

THE EXORCISM

Art.......
It's 5 am and she's still not home
Hehehehe

Once again, I find myself in this cocoon of horror....
Unwanted, familiar place

My most undesirable foe
Possessor of addicts
Professor of manipulation
Habitual line crossing instigator

I denounce you by your horrendous name!
ALCOHOLISM..........

Demoralizing the souls of the weak
Tainting the purity of our love
I must put an end to this, once and for all

As Art prepares for battle, he has no idea that his alter ego Arturo is on his way to double team the enemy. Far from unscathed, scarred by the battle wounds of 25 years of spiritual warfare, he is determined to save his family. Blessed with the ammunition of ADVERSITY, the sword of SANCTUARY. Nurtured by the words of the GOOD BOOK, armed with an unlimited supply of bullets of FAITH, holy water of HOPE, grenades of REDEMPTION. Ready to open fire upon the Demon with a barrage of steroidal Angels, equipped with repertoires

and resumes of destroying evil and restoring faith.
Let us begin....

IN THE NAME OF CHRIST, SHOW YOURSELF!

The demon whistles Mary had a little lamb..........

AUDACIOUS ALIENATOR
PRINCE OF PERJURY
BARRON OF BROKEN HEARTS

HAHAHAHA!

CHASTISER OF CONTRIDICTION
DESTROYER OF HOPE
DEVOURER OF DREAMS

Arturo is dead!
He's with us!

YOU HAVE NO AUTHORITY OVER MY
LIFE, AND NEVER WILL!
IN THE NAME OF CHRIST, I CAST YOU OUT!
YOU HEARTLESS HEATHEN!

The Demon's strength is undeniable as Art attempts to pry the enemy's diabolical clutches off his family

What makes you think I will ever leave you alone?
I cursed you with insecurity, lies, adultery,
spitting my venom of hopelessness and corruption in the

face of your love. I will infect her until she rots on this earth, like the dirty scoundrel she is, as you once were, still are...
Just give up Art before I have you both again, and next time you won't escape.

MASTER MANIPULATOR!

Fuck you Art!
Arturo isn't here to save your ass!

DEMON OF DESTRUCTION!
BEAST OF BRUTALLITY!

You're not man enough for her!
She doesn't love you, she loves me!

FACE OF FECALITY!

You know where she's at?

IN THE NAME OF CHRIST, I REBUKE YOU!

Fake ass Christian
You're a joke
Your book sucks!

FOR THE LAST TIME, STAY THE FUCK AWAY FROM HER! BE GONE! YOU PLAYER HATER FROM HELL!

You weak minded, misguided believer. I will continue to torment your marriage; I am the chink in the armor of your soul that will never go away. Soon, you will be defenseless to my tortuous persecution, as I impregnate her body with the seed of swine, hypnotizing her with my criminal mind.

DEVOTEE OF LIES AND PERVERSION!
UNWANTED INFILTRATOR!
BE GONE!
I CAST YOU BACK TO THE DEEPEST, DIRTIEST DEPTHS OF THE ABYSS!

THE POWER OF POSITIVITY COMPELS YOU!
THE POWER OF HOPE COMPELS YOU!

She can't stand you!
You can't trust her!

THE POWER OF REDEMPTION COMPELS YOU! THE POWER OF THE LOVE FOR MY WIFE, COMPELS YOU! THE POWER OF CHRIST COMPLELS YOU!

Oh, shit!
Arturo?
WTF!
What's he doing here!

THAT'S RIGHT PUTO, I'M BACK!

Damn you!
Demons retreat!

YOU UGLY, BAD BREATH DEMONIC DICKHEAD.
LORD HAVE MERCY ON THIS PREDATOR OF
ADDICTION, AS IT KNOWS NO BETTER.

As the Demon flies away in defeat, Art and Arturo notice one of his wings is damaged from the affliction of their tag team assault. Right before he disappears back to the Abyss, he looks back and says............

You might have won the battle, but the war is far from over. So until next Thursday, my favorite foe, my old friend.
Just remember one thing....
She's madly in love with me; put that in your book!

Hahahahahahaha!

HIGH ROAD

Face swollen, from the constant slaps, as I turn the other cheek, time and time again
Bleeding tongue, taking bite after bite
The price I pay, having a heart of gold
All this, driving down the high road

LOVE LESS

You were once the girl of my dreams
Why do you continue to haunt me?
We were very much in love
After high school sweethearts
The beauty queen of queens
Hated on, because I was your king
Then one day you broke my heart
My life shattered to pieces
Soul torn apart
Confused
As you continued to love me, even though you loved another…
Deep down inside, I know it's wrong
Loving me one day, the next day you're gone
I take what I can get
A BITTER SWEET TREAT
Love less…
To say the least

ONLY IN MY DREAMS

So ten years later you realize that I'm the one
But I'm married now
Daughter and son
Tempted
Reminiscing
Scarred
As your beauty set an unrealistic bar
Always wondered if this time would come
It came
Now I'm forced to run
What could have been?
What could be?
An affair
That remains to be seen

Still lovers…
But only in my dreams

AND

All you care about is your writing!
That's all you do, and pray….
It's pathetic…..

And?

TORN

The moments I share with both of you I can't compare
Two lovers
My heart split in two…
Is this a blessing?
It doesn't feel right
Is this a test?
It doesn't feel wrong
My conscience I fight…
Two lovers
My heart split in two…

What would you do?

PHYCHO!

Why do you get so angry with me?
Phycho!
You're freaken crazy!

Calm down baby….
I get mad because I love you

THE GODFATHER

Thank you Godfather for helping me in my time of need.
I appreciate you
Don't thank me, thank Abi
I'm doing this for the kids
Now get your life together and make us proud

I will

CAN OF WORMS

The deeper I get into this book; I realize I've opened up a can of spiritual worms. The enemy has taken notice, as I'm engaged in a full on spiritual war.......
Having second thoughts about this
The characters are starting to consume my soul
Real talk

THE LINE

Undeniable spark
I know you feel the same…
Nervous
Intoxicated lust
Flustered
A dangerous game…
Built up
Hoping
Finally, it's time….

My finger on the trigger…
But again, I can't cross the line

MIRROR

Mirror mirror on the wall
Why do haters hate?

Haters gonna hate

LAST DANCE

You came at a time I needed you most
Unexpectedly, you stole my heart….
Embezzled my mind
Seduced my spirit
But we both love another…

Ridiculed by thoughts of regret
It's you; I want to sow my oats
Thinking to myself; what would Pac do?
Feeling ashamed…
Am I wrong for hoping there's a chance?
Or in denial
That this is my last dance

LEFT OUT

Fish out of water……..
Dehydrating from loneliness
Suffocated by rejection
Desperate, as I look in from the outside

FLATLINED

Lord, please give me a sign
Something to keep me going
My heart is flat lined_____

Can't shake this depression
My faith I question

To the delight of my ears, I hear my daughter's voice
DADDY!

__/___/___/___/___/___/___/___/___/___/\

IS THAT YOU?

Are you that gorgeous sunrise that greets me every day with my cup of coffee and morning prayer?
Or the guardian angel that keeps my family out of harms way……..
Is she that helping hand that comes out of nowhere and pulls my head out of the clouds when I'm confused

Is that you?

ME

Anointee of the ANOINTER
Son of the ORANGE ROSE
Jr to a SAINT
Stepson to the GODFATHER
Sibling to the SHOOTING STARS
Father of DIAMONDS
Husband to the QUEEN OF FIRE….
Member of the DREAM TEAM
Manos de PIEDRA
Disciple of PAC
Wannabee like MIKE
Influencer of LOVE
Foe of HATE
Evader of EVIL
Searcher of FATE
Possessee of THE WORD
Possessor of WISDOM
Professor of FAITH
Philosopher of HOPE
Creator of DOPE POETRY…
Road to REDEMPTION
Mind of MALISHA
Body of ZEUS
Soul of CAPONE
Heart of GOLD

SOLDADO DE LA VIDA

ARTURO

Big heart
Good soul
Old school
Addicted to women and blow
Kurtis Blow, that's what I meant….
He's playing basketball…
He loves that basketball…

ANOINTED…
Got the glow
Fighting Sho Nuff
Doesn't hate
Doesn't lie…
Getting high, watching time fly

Positive thinker
Cool and calm
Disappointed his mom
Driving his family crazy
Trying to change his ways
Searching for better days

He found Jesus!
Got humbled
Tied the knot, had two kids
Oh, I'm sorry
He did it backwards
Had two kids
Found Jesus
Tied the knot

Got humbled....

Family getting stronger
Days getting longer
Writing dope stories...
Smoking dope
Feeling dope
Spirit strong
Physical beast
Money tight
Never right...
Walking the walk
Talking the talk
Battling demons
Real talk

Captain of the ship
Stacking chips
Just an OG, trying to learn new tricks
Real shit........

Big appetite for
God
Family
Money, Booty and Pho
In that order

Faith is tested every single second
Each and every hour
Hourglass running out of sand
Trying to understand...

This super, duper
Mutherfucken
Supercalifragilisticexpialidocious
Scary
No trust
No love
Junkie infested
Feel sorry for non-believing
Gold digging
Fake booty
Fake society, everything fake, fake, fake!
Jake the snake!

Addiction to porn
Addiction to drugs
Addiction to likes......

Blasphemous world leaders
Cheaters
Bottom feeders
Rumor starters
War starters
Trouble starters
Criminal records
The Lakers record...
Record breaker haters
Player haters
All haters in general
Negative energy
Negative impact
Negative Nancy
Killers...

Not enough leaders
Not enough believers…
One more time
Not enough leaders
Not enough believers…

As Pac sings his solo in the church choir up in heaven
We all look up with hope

Come with me, Hail Mary nigga
Run quick see
What do we have here now?
Do you wanna ride or die?
Ladadadadadadada……

Crazy thing called life

WOMEN

Can't live with them…
Can't love without them

MY SONG

My thoughts throw you down like Byron Russell
The last shot
At winning your love
3, 2, 1!
Arturo again! YES!
Oh, a spectacular move by Arturo Barcinas!

Mesmerizing your mind
Seducing your curiosity
Serenading your soul
Your eyes are suddenly addicted to my words……
As I express myself to you on this canvas called life
Like Picasso I continue to flow
Not about my highs
All about my lows
The low writer, that's me
Rolling in my imaginary 64
Leaving myself vulnerable to the opinionated creatures
Creatures of doubt
Creatures of fear
As I take you on my unstable roller coaster ride…..
No seatbelts allowed
Locked in my world
Possessed by my positive spirit
Exorcism not an option…
I force you to submit
As you contradict your original views of my words,
and your fascination with trying to persuade your mind about
your own insecurities and self-doubts……
The sun continues to shine though my magnifying glass,

zapping haters and disbelievers like ants
As we fly together through the heavens like Superman and Lois Lane……
But I don't have an S on my chest
I wear my heart on my chest
Caught in the crossfire of SPIRITUAL WAR….
We finally land in heaven
My mother greets us with a kiss
Just a taste, a sample of what we have to miss
Strategizing redemption
Mastering forgiveness
Sharpening my blade
Cutting the fat off the fat lady
As she tries to tell me how to sing my song?
Shit…………
A song that will continue
Even when I'm gone

Drop the mic

DAMN

Basking in the calm of the storm, reflecting on my last encounter with the enemy….
I can't help but notice the angry thunder clouds on the Horizon……
Damn, here we go again

SENSITIVITY

As the enemy stews in defeat, wounded from our last encounter…
I find it odd, how sensitive and vulnerable she has become

PATHS

Our paths cross again
A secret, innocent love
More than a friend…
Every time we meet, our hearts don't skip a beat
Same song
Same line
Oh well…
Until we meet again

POPS

I have the most peaceful, honest, loving father in the world.
Thanks POPS for teaching me what love is, and setting a
perfect example of what a man is. If I haven't told
you lately, I love you……

ROUND 99

As I limp to my corner; wounded by the devastating barrage
of destruction the enemy has inflicted in his latest attempt to
take my soul…
Jesus fixes my cuts, heals the swelling, and says

Stay strong Art; I'm in your corner mijo
You've trained for eternal life…
Ding Ding Ding! Round 100!

THE ESE IN ME

CHALE HOLMES!
Me llamo Arturo
Some call me El Guapo
Others call me El Gato
Getting frisky with the heinas
Stomping all the ratons
El Gran Campeon
Throwing up the W…
I'm from Wilmington
D St. Holmes!
The baddest ese on the block
Arturo from the block
One hand on my Bible
The other on my glock…
Dikies, wife beater and house slippers
Never slippin'….
Pop locking like Rerun
What's happening!
Jamming to oldies
I'm your puppet
Acting classes with Big Puppet
Real shit
American, Mexican, Filipino, Chamorro, ME!
Wilmas on my chest…
Always stressed
Sweated by the five-o
Rolling in my imaginary 64
A suspect for a 187
Guilty of a 5150….
I got 99 problems

But the pinta aint one!

No tattoo tears

Shedding tears, as I get my Picasa of Alicia on my back,

RIP Mama

The OG's have my back

A street ball legend, they call me MJ

The Mexican Jordan (what can I say)☺

Soccer on Sundays after church with the mojados

Mi ruca looking fine, sipping on mojitos

Goal!!!!!!!!!!!!!!!!!!!!!!!!!!!!!!!!!!

As I score another goal

Accomplishing goals

Coaching FUTBOL

Writing books

The low writer, that's me…

Slap boxing mi mijo

Duran vs. Mando Ramos

Vamanos!

Its la huda!

Time to go!

Diamond in the front

Sun roof down

Kicking it in the scene

I'm a gangster of God

A feign for love…

For hope…

For peace in mi barrio……………

As my girl Rosie and the originals takes us home

Good night and God bless you all…

Angel baby… my angel baby….

NO JOKE

Anticipation of completing my book has definitely giving me strength. At the same time, I feel like I'm throwing gas in the fire. The enemy is outraged, as the Dream Team is building up the church and getting stronger and stronger every day…..
I know the battle is far from over though….
Crossfire of spiritual war is no joke……

CHOICES

Once a liar, always a liar
Once a cheater, always a cheater
If they choose to be

ADDICTS PRAYER

I hope I die before I wake
Too much suffering
Soo much too take
Can't cope
No hope
Need help
Need dope
No I don't

Where's Jesus?
Head in a daze
Heart cut in half
Need help
As Satan laughs....
No you don't

ICEMAN

Crept, into my society like a thief in the night
My people hooked, and that ain't right...
Breaking bread
Breaking hearts
Breaking bad…
A filthy demon
Sick
The devil's dick…
Ruthless
Killing souls
Toothless...
Glorified
Walter White
Faces of meth
Faces of death…
Continuous struggle
Uphill fight...
Darkness
Hopeless
No love
No glory...
Till meth do us part
End of story…

RIP

He was the life of the party
But a casualty to reality

FIRE

Her energy was wild and inappropriate…
Her spirit, ruthless and uncontrollable…
Her mind confused and corrupt…
But the sex was fire

MAN OF GOD

Somewhat flawed
Sometimes weak
Always vulnerable
Love I seek…
Confused
A bit of doubt
A man of God
I'll be alright…

Just another day
A continuous fight…

THEY

They met
They loved
They lived
They had a boy!

They struggled
They lied
They cheated
They split☹

They couldn't live without each other

They found Jesus!
They had a girl!
They wed
They love
They live
They struggle
They have faith
They believe

To be continued……………….

DOES SHE LOVE ME?

She loves me, she loves me
She loves me, she loves me not….
She loves me not, she hates me
She hates me, she despises me
She calls for me, she makes love to me
She loves me, she loves me not
She hates me, she hurts me
She almost kills me…..
Real talk…..
She tries to leave me……
She can't……..
She loves me, she loves my poetry
She makes love to me, again and again
She is my soulmate, wife and inspiration
She drives me crazy……
But she love me

DANCER AND THE POET

He was connected at her hip, Waltz partners for life
The moon was her disco ball
The galaxy her dance floor

She's the star of his show….
Lead role in his novel….
A novel that has yet to be completed
To be continued….

YOUNG AND BEAUTIFUL

Sexy, charismatic with no sense of time
Everything was easy
Life loving her to the fullest….
For this was her time to shine
A time she will never forget
The time she was young and beautiful

ONE OF THOSE NIGHTS

It was a magical night, a modern day romance for the ages
As they painted the town like Picasso's Les Demoiselles d'Avignon....
Danced the night away, like it was their last.....
Made love under the stars till they collapsed in each other's arms....
It was a night, that makes life worth living

MIRROR MIRROR

Mirror mirror on the wall
How come my life is so difficult?
What did I do to deserve this?

You didn't do anything Art
But unfortunately, the cloth you were cut from is discontinued.......
Good hearts are on the verge of extinction
Lovers are now the minority
Don't be so hard on yourself
That's just where we're at

Thanks mirror

Don't mention it

WHEN I GO

When it's time for me to go
I want my people to know
That I'm in a better place…
A place where it's all good……………
Whether you're from the bright lights of the big city
Or from the ghetto streets of the hood…………
A place where the confused and misguided are understood…
All love
No hate
A place where we all, JUST GET ALONG

So don't be mad
Because I'm in a special place
A place where there's no killers
No drugs
No liars
No tears
No fears
Where everybody knows your name…
And they're always glad you came…
Like cheers
A place where there's no hunger
No crying babies
No junkies
No hookers
No pimps
A place women are treated like QUEENS

All we do is win
No sin
No debts
No regrets
No rich or poor
A place where it's all for the better
And never for worse

So don't be sad
I'm at the place to be…..
A place where there are no terrorists or war
No bombs
No wrongs
Just bongs……

Getting high with Bob Marley, as he serenades me

One love……… One Heart……
Let's…. get…. together…. and… feel…. all right

Playing whiffle ball with Babe Ruth
Chilling with Pac, as he preaches the truth
Or dancing with the real star, Jesus
As we C-walk in Heaven together…….

So please, please don't cry when I die
Because I'll be in a much, much better place
flying with my mom, high in the sky….
And to my children and wife

Daddy's an angel now….
Just getting us prepared for heaven and eternal life…….

THE MEETING

We have to stop meeting like this….
People are starting to talk…

Talk about what, your weak ass book, lol
Art, you're an idiot, fooling yourself into thinking you're a writer…
Write about that…..

And you're a liar!

Am I?
Now you're a man of God, all of a sudden…
Shit…..
Good luck with that, you think he's going to make your life easy?

Not easy, just fuller
Full of faith, hope and eternal life, that's what I want
Something I never had with you…

But why?
You got paid to party……..
Arturo was the man….
Liquor, drugs, beautiful women, whenever you pleased

A fantasy, every man's dream…

Not every man….
Fantasy is a fairytale…
Made up of beautiful empty reflections of reality

But the women, you had the best

It was lust, that's all it was, and a lot of broken hearts
The only woman who ever really loved me was my mother; and
I broke her heart. Now that I look back, the only thing I have to
fall back on is a bunch of soulless memories, faceless affairs

You know I'm never going stop torturing you, right?

Why, why me?

Because you're anointed…

That doesn't make sense…

They didn't tell you, did they?

Tell me what?

When you become saved, your life not only becomes more
 difficult than it already is; now you're engaged in a 24 hour, 365
days, until the end of time battle for your soul, and you're on the
clock bitch…

Who you calling bitch?

You…

I understand what you're saying, but this is what I signed up for
The lord is my shepherd, that's where I'm at

Are you happy?

Pause……
Sometimes, sometimes not
But I'm fine with that

Let me ask you?
Your marriage is always on the rocks
The world is not your friend
You have money problems
You're a sex addict…..
Lol, is happiness really what it's all cracked up to be?
I wouldn't want to be you….

Then why are you trying to take my soul?

Because I'm a bottom feeder….
I prey on the low picking of the fruit, easy targets like you
I want to rain on your parade, darken your shine until your corpse lies rotting on this earth
That's what I do…

Good luck with that…

You think singing solo's in church is going to take you to the promise land?
That doesn't exist till someone sees it…

You're banking on stories from a book thousands of years old

I'm here to do my diligence for Jesus; and nothing is going stop me....
Not sex, not drugs, not money, especially not you.....
I see what you're doing; dangling kryptonite carrots in front of my soul.....
Trying to corrupt my family, fuck that, I'm not having it

You weak misguided sheep; running around chasing your tail with the rest of the blessed
You can't even handle your own family.....
Lol, you're a joke

Oh really?

Really....
Let me make you an offer you can't refuse....
Fame, fortune; whatever you desire, it's yours
You came so close last time we were together

I already went that route; it's not for me
I'm in good hands now, God's hands

That pretty pathetic Art
You really trust Jesus that much?
What has he done for you lately?

Yes, it's called faith
He blessed me with a beautiful wife and two healthy kids......

C'mon Art, one more time...

I can't be rolling the dice with you anymore
Yeah, I rolled 7 11s once in a while
But most times I crapped out

Let's cut to the chase…
What's it going to take to win your soul?

Seriously?

What's your price?

My soul is off the market, already spoken for

Boy, JC has you whipped

Yep

What if I leave your wife alone?

I knew you'd bring that up

That's right; she's my bridge to your soul

Lucifer, why don't you just go back to the old you
You were an Angel for crying out loud….
Just bight the bullet and swallow your pride, ask for forgiveness

Fuck that, I pay the cost to be the boss
I am pride….

The boss of who?

The boss of you…..

Art's wife enters the room

Here come's your wife; tell her thanks for last night

**Screw you Lucifer; I'm done with you too…
My husband is the only one for me…
You might have had a strong grasp on me before,
but our days are over….**

Lol, yeah right; that's not what you said last night
How cute, husband and wife
I guess I'm going to have to kill two birds with one stone

No, three of us
Don't forget about Jesus

Lol, watch your backs, I'm not going away that easy, and Art

What?

Do you realize what you're doing?

What…

Writing about us….
You opened up a can of worms you might not be able to close
Let that sink in for a minute…….
You're playing with fire; and we all know how this story ends

COMING SOON

Baring the fruits of my family's labor, I'm given a second chance in life……
As I escape from the world of corruption and sin
My family by my side
In God's hands
Still, no idea where to begin
Trying change my ways
Chasing rainbows and sunny days
Still caught in the eye of the storm
My eyes on the prize
A HAPPY HOME……
As I attempt to live by the laws of the good book
Thinking to myself…
Maybe these laws aren't for me?
Can't think like that
No cheat sheet
As Satan looks over my shoulders
Cutting corners
Getting cut by every corner
Cornered by reality
Scared of my own shadow……….
As I take a second look at my past
Fearful of what the future holds
I share with you my journey of hardship and struggle
My story of re-invention…………
Reestablishing myself for……….. REDEMPTION

                COMING SOON

AFTER OUR FATHER

Our Father prayer x1

Thank you lord for another day
Thank you for turning my financial situation around
Thanks for getting my son through his second year of school, unscathed and showing improvement…..
Thanks for keeping my children happy, and most important, healthy…
Thank you for helping me fight all these damn demons…
Thank you for the world's best family
Thanks for blessing me with the gift of writing, and giving me an outlet to express myself through these crazy days we live in…….
Thank you for my first book, and giving me ammunition for my second………
Thank you for improving my marriage……
Thank you for my beautiful wife, have I told you lately, that I LOVE YOU
Thank you for my future blessings……….
Thank you for getting my family back together through the power of my church, REAL TALK
I can go on and on and on for days……………
I guess what I'm really trying to say is, thank you for being you……
AMEN

BURNT BRIDGES

So many go through life burning bridges
No conscience of consequence
You wonder why we live in this world of flames and burning bridges..........

DISTURBED

As my Goddess sleeps in peace
I lay next to her exhausted, licking my battle wounds from the night before.......
Fearful of what's next
Disturbed, as I find myself excited as well

GODDESS AND THE KING

The Goddess calls for me again....
The stench of her morning's orgasm purposely keeps my senses aroused throughout the day
My face and hands still basting in her marinade....
Adrenalin running wild at the visual of caressing her soft creamy skin....
Taste buds enticed by the treat of her taste
My fingers excited; at the same time corrupt; plotting our next affair
Hands clapping like a toy monkey banging cymbals; symbolizing animalistic, uninhibited desire.......
I insist to be the giver....
The Lioness submits...
That perfect heart shape ass calls my name
Her neck begging my tongue for attention...
Hips glowing in my sheets like a precious gem, instigating my erection.....
I tease her clit with my tip; sap dripping from the solid wood.....
My lips on a one track mind to her curves; exploring each
nook and cranny like Vasco da Gama....
She calls me Maverick as I straddle her from behind, locked in like Top Gun; shooting goose bumps down her spine...
I tickle her from head to toe; licking her from head to toe, kissing her from head to toe, skipping that ass; saving the best for last....
Nibbling her feet like baby corn on the cob; spider fingering her legs; worshipping and kneading that perfect bubble butt like dough; taking my time, doing it right, I'm in the zone......
Exaggerated squirts of oil; lathering her skin like an Aztec Warrior lathers his queen....Possessed by the spirit of a cannibalistic Mandingo; I savagely eat her from behind....

My spirit indulged as my Goddess squirms like a fish out of water; quenching my thirst with her bittersweet treat....
She wants my cock...
Happy trigger fingers on my pistol
Raising eyebrows, as I rise to the occasion...
Pause......
Her tight pussy ridicules my mind; blows kisses to my soul, sings love songs to my heart
As I tear it apart.......
Euphoria in the air, stimulated cupids, dilated pupils, high from the fumes of our ardor....
Changing speeds, she shifts my gears, trying not to bust
She looks back at me; slow down baby, no need to rush...
This is yours, till death do us part.
Sky rocket in flight, absolute delight.....
Built up, fearing the end like Armageddon
The moon, the sun, the stars aligned in perfect harmony
I'm ready to erupt...
The twinkle in her eyes, twinkle in my toes; attempting to tip toe around the storm....
Hoping I can bite the bullet, dodge the bullet......
But it feels too good; I'm hit, man down!
As Eros, the God of Love escapes from my body reincarnated as a spirited unforgiving tsunami of rapture....
Drenching the goddess with a downpour of bliss...
She stews in the aftermath like a cub stews in honey; savoring each drop like it's the last...
I lay exhausted, licking my paws; comforting my love as we collapse in each other's arms...........
I can't help but think to myself; damn, it's good to be the King

The end

I UNDERSTAND

I understand why some men leave their families; it's hard to be a good daddy....
I understand why we get hooked on dope; fucked up shit happens every second.
I understand why we steal and kill; we live on an unleveled playing field.............
I understand why we commit suicide; LIFE'S A BITCH
I understand why we lie; the truth hurts like a muthafucker......
I understand why haters hate; no I don't
I understand why they stare; because I look good.......
I understand why we cheat; temptation is a good friend of mine......
I understand why we have a crazy ass, ruthless president; we live in a crazy ass ruthless world.....
I understand why the women love me; that's just the way it is......
I understand why I can't write about fairytales; fairytales are just fairytales.......
I understand why we don't trust cops; no comment
I understand why prejudice still exists; somethings will never Change...
I understand why we don't believe in God; because you choose not to.... I'm not mad at cha
I understand I'm blessed with the gift of writing; because I got it from my mama... real talk
I understand that the enemy is on my ass; because I'm ANOINTED...
I understand that I'm in a spiritual war; a battle for my soul......

I understand it's not easy being me; my genetic makeup
consists of Angels, Saints and Godfathers who all love
and support me; I don't want to disappoint them anymore
I understand my life is an open book; I'm sharing my
TESTIMONY
I understand I'm fortunate to have an audience; I just hope
you understand
Comprende?

THERAPY

The more she engages in my story
She realizes the star of the show is her
My writing seems to be therapeutic to her soul…
That being said, gives me inspiration to write more

MY SEED

Continuous battle
A strategic game of one on one VS myself
Questioning my intelligence
Testing my patience
When I look at you
I see my eyes
I realize; you are me
I am you
A better version of me
I will sculpt you to be
With GOD, positive energy and LOVE
You will succeed
My first, my son
My seed

YOU FORCED ME

You came at a time that wasn't fair
Daddy's lowest point
Soul in despair.......
My precious baby girl is here....
Did my mother come back as you?
Because like her....
You forced me to love at a time my heart didn't want to love.....
Feel at a time I couldn't feel
To revive
You forced me to be your daddy

MIRROR

Mirror mirror on the wall
Who is the luckiest dad of them all?

You are Arturo……..
Loving, healthy, beautiful children are a true blessing
Don't ever take that for granted

I won't

BAE

All this time, I've made love to your body
But neglected your soul
Abandoned your heart
I didn't feel your pain
Kicked you when you were down
Didn't listen to your cries for help
I was too concerned about getting my own life on track
I forgot we are one
Husband and wife
I'm sorry my love….
I promise I will never leave you alone again

MY BAD

I know the first time wasn't quite what you imagined, my love……
You deserved more
No knee to the floor
Then my whole world went crashing down☹
Happy ten-year anniversary baby
I promise I will make it up to you

THE MAKE UP

My inspiration
I cry for your attention
Beg for you affection……
The prize in my eyes, you are to me……..

The starring role in my book
You sexy butterfly that stings like a bee
Baby………

Will you marry me?

OG TEN COMMANDMENTS

1. Don't get hooked on dope; I mean crack and meth MJs ok
2. Don't talk the talk, unless you walk the walk
3. Treat women with respect, like you treat your mother
   If they deserve it, because some of you are crazy
4. Don't bullshit, ain't no one got time for that
5. Stay loyal to the good people in your corner, we are the minority...
6. Be humble, all this glitz and glam don't mean a thing come judgment day...............
7. Never bite the hand that feeds you, ever
8. Stay away from another man's wife, serious repercussions are involved.............
9. Position yourself properly, don't put yourself in bad predicaments.....

Last but not least, the most important commandment

10. Take care of your kids, be there for them

LIKE ME

Daddy, when I grow up, I want to be just like you
Mijo, come sit on my lap real quick
Let me tell you something young blood…..
You can be anything you want to be
Like Mike
A preacher man
Platinum artist…
El Presidente
Just don't ever let me hear you say you want to be like me
Now run along youngster……..

Ok daddy

BEAUTIFUL MIND

I can't remember her face
But her mind……
Her mind was beautiful

THE RIGHT TRAIN

For your safety, remain seated with your hands, arms, feet, and legs inside the train, and watch your children please

Para su seguridad, permanezca sentado con las manos, brazos, pies, y piernas dentro el tren. Y cuida a tus niños. Por favor.

Hello everyone, my name is Art and I am your tour guide. My alter ego Arturo is the conductor. Welcome to the RIGHT TRAIN. Please follow these 3 simple rules while on board. 1. No sadness 2. No pain allowed and 3. No blazing up till we get to BLAZE ISLAND…. Turn off your phones, open up your minds, and enjoy the ride……….

ALL ABOARD, THE RIGHT TRAIN! CHOO! CHOO!

As the train takes off, we notice that a group of young Angles through the rear window challenging us to a friendly race. It's a beautiful sight.

Our first stop, the FIELDS OF JOY

Arturo has the train bumping, going full throttle, right before they pull up to the first stop. His mother Abi surprises him; he lost her 3 years ago and couldn't wait till they would be together again. Hi my love! She gives him a kiss, a kiss he missed.

Arturo is in total shock and disbelief, he puts the train on cruise control, gives her a big kiss and squeezes her like he's never letting her go. He asks her for a dance, the dance at his wedding they never had. The whole train shedding tears of joy, clapping, and forming a circle around them as Eydie Gorme performs her classic, Sabor a Mí, which happens to be Abi's favorite song. She tells him; I'm proud of you son. The way you turned your life around and kept the family together, I had no doubt in my mind that when I left, you would be the spiritual leader of the familia. Now quit crying and let's dance. Oh yeah, I love your book mijo, it's beautiful.

The FIELDS OF JOY have always been Arturo's personal favorite; he helped build it from scratch. It was built for everyone who had a heavy heart on Earth. So you figure, it's one of our most popular destinations. It's the place that grows unlimited amounts of the PERMITTED FRUIT. The fruit that gives us faith and forgiveness. The fruit the Angles take to keep their wings shiny. Rejuvenated from his mother's presence, Arturo has a gleam in his eyes we've never seen before, a smile from ear to ear. All was good in the FIELDS OF JOY

Next stop, BLAZE ISLAND…….

Right before we pull up we see a positive cloud of JOY on the horizon. The host Bob Marley greets us with his smash hit; I WANNA LOVE YA AND TREAT YOU RIGHT…. Blaze Island is another big favorite. It's the place Jesus grows his universally famous JC KUSH….

A magical flower that gives us strength, hope, and imagination.
A flower that was misused and mistreated on Earth. Here in Heaven, it's our national plant and part of our national pastime, LOVE AND HAPPINESS............

The passengers were Chinese eyed, laughing, singing and dancing in pure glee. Arturo and his mom danced for hours and hours, crying and reminiscing about the good old days...... But for some reason, he couldn't stop crying... Wiping his tears, he takes a few deep breaths, rolls up his sleeves, sticks out his chest.......

The next stop, THUG MANSION

This is where all the Gangsters of God stay. Hosted by Arturo's favorite poet 2PAC, who just texted him; were ready for you. This was a sacred place for Arturo; most of his people reside here, friends, family, and many of his role models. It seems like most of the OGs call this place home. Arturo loves Pac though, he looked forward to spending quality time with him, writing and critiquing each other's work; pushing one another to the highest level possible. The level of HEAVENLY GLORY.....
Pac praised Arturo on his book CROSSFIRES OF SPIRITUAL WAR, which he had a starring role in. Right before we left, Arturo took a selfie with Biggie, Pac, Sinatra, Bruce Lee, Ali and Elvis, it was a special sight.

The anticipation of the LAST STOP had the passengers in a frenzy of JUBILATION. The place we all came to see.

LAST STOP, JCs MAGICAL PLAYGROUND!

The star of the show, the box office sensation. The place we all wanted to be, next to the man, the myth, the legend, the one who died for our sins back on earth................

As we gather around the MESSIAH, he shares beautiful stories of his time on earth and how he will always love and protect us. He breaks bread and a magical feast appears right before our eyes, quenches our thirst with REDEMPTIONAID; serenades us to his favorite chapters of the GOOD BOOK. What more could we ask for? After multiple group selfies; Jesus pulls Arturo aside and says, I just want you to know, I'm proud of you, the way you got your shit together and took care of your family.
One more thing, I love your book............

I appreciate that my Lord, thanks for blessing me with the gift of writing.

Still ecstatic from JCs comments, Arturo COULD BELIEVE how awesome his day was. Right after the tour finished, he went straight to his mother and held her tighter than he's ever held anything in his life. He finally felt complete. He's with his mommy again.....
This time, forever....

Just another day on the RIGHT TRAIN........
CHOO! CHOO!

HEAVEN'S DOOR

No 6 by 8, no bars
Incarcerated on an unleveled playing field, that's where we are
Beaten on an unbeaten path…
Fuck Armageddon this is hell
Ain't no sunshine when he comes……………
Trapped in a society that's made up from a society of scandalous tyrants, voted in by our people………
Let me repeat that, voted in by our people
We win some, we lose some, we lose some more
Losing conscience
Losing sight…
Mover and shaker, shaking and baking
Burnt to a crisp, from the heat of our world…
Ridiculed by false profits
Profiting off small minds and corrupted souls….
In the meantime; my heart continues to grow
My words continue to flow…
The enemy continues his work…
His eyes on the prize, my soul…..
Searching for a fix………
Rather be judged by one, then carried by triple six…
My Spidey senses always tingling
Zapping webs of redemption at haters and disbelievers
Jesus on my mind full time…
I tried part time, but it didn't work…
It's hard to be a full time Man of God….
When my life consists of, fulltime man, fulltime husband, full time poet and overtime dad…..
My wife and kids my inspiration
Gangster of God my aspiration

Fighting with weapons of demonic destruction
Shielded by the Angel's wings….
My mother looks down upon me from heaven
Smiling at her son; singing solos of redemption
Praying it's not too late for reinvention
At the same time; in serious need of intervention…..
This ain't Mr. Rodgers neighborhood
This is Arturo's hood
Venting life through my words
Crossfire of Spiritual War….
It's the end of the world, and I know it…
And I don't feel fine….
While the rich get richer
The poor get violent….
Loyalty and devotion out of reach
Playing Frisbee with temptation and addiction……
Morality no longer the curriculum
Corruption and self-destruction I continue to fight
Praying one day I'll see the light
As these walls cave in on me more and more……and more….
All this on the high road to eternal life
AKA Heaven's door

THE LEGEND

The ace is back..........
Flying high like an eagle through the sea of redemption
That's where I'm at
Coming out the gates like #24 1/22/06
I got 81 problems
But loves not one.....
Doing the mamba with the queen of fire
Eternal life, that's my desire
Singing lead on Sundays with my people
Giving love to my people
My people love me..........
They love when I write about reality and our everyday struggle.....
All witnesses
As I testify about my pain and glory
Waiting to hear my next story.......
Saved
Reborn
Taking the corporate world by storm
Survived a corporate economic storm
As the good book remolds my heart like clay
I mean what I say
Talking loud like Cassius Clay
Give me that OG from J
As I serenade your lady today......
Super dad
My aka
One hand on my bible
The other on my AK
47 right around the block

Blocking all the disbelievers and naysayers like Mutumbo
Waving my finger
GET THAT SHIT OUT OF MY HOUSE!
Late blooming
As my seeds blossom through the fields of joy
Hot child in my city
Running wild with the queen of fire
Haters mad, cause we still look pretty
Can't be like Mike
Can give a fuck about likes
I'm lying about that one, lol
Captain of my team
Ball in my hands
Against the clock
Double, triple, sometimes quadruple teamed
Crossing haters over like AI
No more Mr. Nice guy……….
As the world takes my kindness for weakness
Coming back
MAS GRANDE
MAS FUERTE
MAS RAPIDO
Main events against the enemy
Jesus in my corner
Fixing my cuts
Healing the swelling before I get a big head…….
As this mutherfucken demon tries to wear me down
Down goes Satan, down goes Satan!
Another KO
I can't trust a decision…….
And did I mention?
The undisputed, undefeated, defending

Champion of REDEMPTION………
Manos de piedra
El gran campion
Arturo Barcinas…………
The man, the myth, the legend

MIRROR

Mirror mirror on the wall
Who is the most handsome of them all?

Your son is……
Keep him humbled
Teach him right
Don't let him grow up making the same mistakes you made

Word…….

SOMEBODY

To be
Or not to be….
That's the question we all have to ask
Everybody trying to be a somebody
But who's to say
Who is?
Who's what?
Who's not?
Who's who?
Acting a fool
Trying to be cool…
Just act right
That's all you have to do
Quit trying to be a somebody
Just be you

MVP (most valuable poet)

Bottom of the 9th
The words of wisdom down 4-1
2 outs
Bases loaded….
Now batting
#23
Arturo Barcinas…….
The crowd roars…….
MVP! MVP! MVP!
First pitch; swing and a miss, strike one!
Second pitch; curve ball on the outside, ball one
Third pitch; crack! A towering shot to left!
Going, going….
Foul ball!
One and two
The next pitch; knuckle ball low
Two and two
The enemy out of the stretch
The pitch; oh shit!
Right at his head!
He shakes it off
Digs in deep……..
Down 4-1
Bases loaded
Full count…….
The pitch……..
100 mph fastball!
Kaboom!
He takes it to dead center!
Going, going!

Gone!
Grand slam!
Hold up, the ball's still going!
Out of the park, into heaven!

The crowd roars!
MVP! MVP! MVP!

QUENCHED

Thirsty bitches…….
For love
Money
Attention
Likes, wtf?
Lol
I admit, I'm guilty of all that
But some of us keep drinking out the wrong glass
Sipping Satan's juice
While Jesus has his lemonade stand posted right in front
I'll take an xlarge glass please……….
Damn, that's delicious
Thank you Lord for quenching my thirst once again
That's where I'm at….

CRITIQUED

I appreciate your opinion
I really do
As you critique my words
Analyze my thoughts
Straight shooter
Shooting off all your opinions
That's what you do…..
But, telling me how to write my stories, through your mind, in your words?

GET THE F#CK OUT OF HERE……….

HE LOVES ME

He loves me…
He loves me lots

BEHIND THE DOOR

Disturbed by the whispering of lies and betrayal
I could hear my wife's soul screaming for help from behind the door
Frightened, at the same time excited
Adrenalin racing
Heart beating frivolously; from the whispers of my names
Arturo…. Art…. Low Writer…. El Gran Campion…Manos de Piedra….MVP
It's him, yes, it's all of them
They're here…….
My hands shaking like I've been electrocuted by 1000 volts of negative energy
Palms sweating
Finally, I build up the courage to open the door……
Greeted by a horrible, disgusting scent words can't describe
Pitch black…………..
Right away I realized where I was, as the door slams shut behind me…
I fall to my knees and pray

Please Lord, get me out of here
Sorry for putting myself in this predicament
Help me, I promise it won't happen again….

Even though I couldn't see, I could feel the evil forces making their way towards me……
Talking shit
Bringing up my past
My soul disappointed, giving me the cold shoulder
Heart wounded, concerned of flat line

Spirit weeping, like an infant crying for his mother
My pen blind folded, held hostage at gun point
Thinking to myself, damn, I can't believe I'm here, again…
As the evil forces slither upon me, wrapping me up like a python coils his prey
I accept defeat……….

To be continued

THE ENEMY

Arturo's coming up
Let's get him

BEHIND THE DOOR PART 2

The demons sang and danced
Out of tune, no rhythm
They bragged amongst each other
The Alcoholic demon was the happiest
Laughing out loud, talking shit

I knew he'd be back
I told him
Lol!
His wife loves me

Fuck that!

I thought that might ring a bell!
Hahaha

All of a sudden!
Like a thief in the night!
Jesus comes blasting in like Biggie Smalls!
Kicking in the door, waving the 44
All we heard was Jesus don't hit me no more…..
Frantically I flick on the light switch
It was a crazy sight; the demons scattered like a frenzy of discombobulated, dysfunctional, tweaking cockroaches
To my bitter surprise, I saw the old me in the crowd
This wasn't my finest hour………
I ran out of the room like Usain Bolt
Relieved, as Jesus was in the hall waiting for me

He says, you know better Arturo
How could you jeopardize losing everything?
You're lucky I love you

Thank you Jesus
I'm just trying to protect my family

I can hear the Alcoholic demon still talking shit behind the Door

I'll see you soon
Don't forget about our little secret
Hahahaha!

Jesus shakes his head
You need to nip that demon in the bud
He's like a wart on your soul
He'll never go away until your wife gets clean

The demon continued to gloat

He's right!
Hahahaha!
I bet your putting this story in your book, right?
Make sure I get my royalties this time
Or better yet, pay me back with the QUEEN OF FIRE
She can cover all your debt

Fuck you asshole!
I don't owe you shit!
I'm not scared of you
I'll beat you like I did last time!

I'll be waiting…………..
As the demon makes his way into the hall

All of a sudden with thunderous force!
Jesus whips the demon with his Father's belt!

The demon cries out like a little bitch
Sorry I won't fuck with him anymore!
Have mercy!

Quit being a hater, leave Arturo alone
One more thing you filthy rodent

Bitch don't kill my vibe!
He shoots the demon back to the abyss with his slingshot of salvation
It was a beautiful sight……..
That's how it's done
I guess you can't ask a sinner to a God's job
Right?

Sorry Lord

It's ok
Remember, I died for your sins

We interrupt your program to bring you this important announcement….

Pray

PAID DUES

No time to reflect
Everything on the fly
Feeling guilty when I'm high, high, high, high
Staying alive, staying alive
Just an OG trying to do it right
I write about the fight
Play by play
Blow for blow
If you don't know, now you know……….
Aspiring to inspire
Scandalous times
Still in my prime
No thought to retire
Respecting my elders
Coming to the conclusion I'm almost an elder
Mentoring my mentors
Real talk…..
Tempted by the tempters
Evading the pretenders
Borderline insane
Life in the fast lane, pumping the brakes
Got no time for the haters
I'm heavy in the game
I want to be a Christian please
But the bitches and demons keep on calling me
Sorry; but I have to refuse
Suckas don't realize, I paid my dues

3 STEPS TO RECOVERY

1. Pray
2. Have faith
3. Believe

COCKTAIL

Our love consists of
1 oz. of lust
2 shots of crazy
A dash of sugar
Shaken, not stirred
Always on the rocks

THE MAIN EVENT

Hello everyone, and welcome to the Positive Energy Center in the gates of Heaven
My name is Art Barcinas and I am your commentator for tonight's fight
We have a 3 round match, for the undisputed championship of redemption

The crowd roars as the anticipation of this match has been brewing for a while. These two fighters absolutely despise each other. You talk about good vs. evil, well here you go. We have a special treat for you, singing the national anthem; we have none other than the King himself, Elvis Pressley. The crowd goes wild for the King as he sings the national anthem beautifully. The King is a big fan of the Champ, vice versa
The crowd roars! MVP, MVP, MVP!
Here we go folks!
Boo......................!
Here comes the challenger, the demon struts in with a cocky attitude, no humility, talking shit. Behind him is Richard Ramirez and Jeffrey Dahmer, the crowd starts praying as pure undeniable evil has made way in the house. The house Arturo built.
Here comes the Champ, 2pac and both of his grandfathers leading him in. Pac performing his hit AMBITIONS OF A WRITER..........

LET'S GET READY TO RUMBLE............!
3 rounds, for the undisputed champion of redemption

Brought to you by, Crossfire of Spiritual War
Sponsored by, the good book
Your referee for tonight is Mills Lane

Here are the rules gentlemen, I mean gentleman……….. No blows below the belt, no biting or kicking. So don't fuck around; I'm firm but fair. The Demon couldn't look Arturo in the eyes, he never has.

    In the black corner
    The challenger
    Boo……………………………..
    Weighing in at 160 lbs
    He is, the master manipulator
    Beast of brutality
    From the depths of hell………………
    The enemy………….
    Boo……………………………!

The crowd roaring, MVP, MVP, MVP!

    In the white corner
    Weighing in at 160 lbs
    From Huntington Beach California………….
    LIBRE CON LIBRE, POUND FOR POUND
    The undisputed, undefeated, defending, champion of
    REDEMPTION……………..
    The crowd roars!
    Manos de Piedra……..
    El gran campeon………..
    The Low Writer……………
    Arturo……………….

Barcinas……………………

The crowd roars MVP, MVP, MVP!
MVP means (most valuable poet).

The bell rings, ding ding ding, round one!
As the fighters meet in the center of the center of ring, the demon right off the bat starts talking shit. The Queen of Fire loves me; she was with me last night. He winks at her and says; I'll see you tonight bae. The Champ responds; you should have never came back, I'll beat ya like I did last time………………
The Champ ignores the scoundrel, works his jab, bobbing and weaving. The enemy throwing vicious combinations to the heart and soul, continuous low blows. Oh shit! The champ already cut, holding on to his soul………. on survival mode…………! The enemy's bone crushing assault seems to be too much for the champ tonight. Arturo keeps pumping the jab though, finally getting his timing down. The demon lands a huge shot to the groin! Down goes Arturo, down goes Arturo!1, 2, 3, 4, 5, 6, 7, 8, 9, ding ding ding! Arturo saved by the bell. Shit, that was close!

Jesus helps Arturo to his corner. Fixing his cuts, healing the swelling, he says; Champ, you need to fight fire with fire, forget the jab, throw left hooks to the ribs. Go to the body, he's soft in the mid-section, he has no legs. Ali in his corner as well; He can't see you, he's too ugly, you're the prettiest OF ALL TIMES!

The challenger has Satan in his corner, GET A BODY BAG, keep going low, keep the pressure on, he's weak. He has no heart, he's done. Hitler and Bin Laden also in his corner; NO MERCY, NO FORGIVENESS, FUCK ARTURO; THAT PAPER CHAMPION!

Arturo looks down at the crowd and sees his wife, the Queen of Fire and his two children. His son yells out, kick his ass daddy! 2pac, Biggie, Sinatra all sitting with the family. Babe Ruth, John Wayne, Edgar Allen Poe, James Dean and Picasso all sitting front row; it was a beautiful sight.

Ding ding ding, round two begins. The Master of manipulation comes out strong, throwing crazy, out of control hay makers. The Champ, floating like a butterfly, stinging like a G, tiring the demon out. The enemy throws him against the corner and unloads a fury of low blows. The Champ playing rope a demon, evading his foul play, and his foul smell. To the delight of the crowd he looks rejuvenated; the chants from his people strengthen his spirit. The presence of his family healing his soul. All of a sudden, he unleashes a furious barrage of clean, precise blows to the demon's body, breaking him down. The crowd going crazy as you can feel the presence of the Holy Spirit in the house. What a fight! The Demon sinking even further, trying to bite the Champ, kicking and still talking shit. The Champ goes wild, while distributing calculated blows to the head and body of the disgusting challenger; at the same time, quoting scriptures of the GOOD BOOK. Ding ding ding, that's the end of round 2. The Demon limps to his corner.

Satan says, listen Alcoholic; Arturo is fighting for his family, you need to find that chink in his armor; we both know what that is. We can't let the both of them get away. I don't give a shit about the belt; our prize is the QUEEN OF FIRE

To the surprise of the Champ, Bruce Lee enters his corner; this is not a charade, you need total concentration, use those strikes I taught you. You got this Champ; put him away and let's party to ALL THIS HEAVENLY GLORY

Ding, ding, ding, round three!
LAST ROUND! Both fighters feeling each other out, cautious. To the surprise of the crowd Teddy Pendergrass starts singing his all-time hit; I'm talking bout a LOVE TKO! The crowd goes wild as the filthy one screams out; I hate that song! No………………..! The champ toying with the challenger, pop shoting at will, not falling for his temptations, performing at a Heavenly level, in full control. The devotee of lies and perversion is out of gas, 10 seconds; the Champ adds one more combination. Ding ding ding, that's the end of the fight!

It's all in the judges hands. Tonight's judges are, Saddam Husain, Martin Luther King Jr and Napoleon. I personally have the fight 2 rounds to 1 for the champ. It should be an easy decision. Let's go to the scorecards

Judge Husain has the bout 3 rounds to none for the Enemy; the crowd boos as the atmosphere in the building was in complete disbelief. Judge King has the bout 30 – 27……. for the Champ; the crowd goes wild; Arturo feeling good about himself. Judge Napoleon has it 2 rounds to one……………..29-28……………..AND STILL…THE UNDISPUTED, UNDEFEATED, CHAMPION OF REDEMPTION

MANOS DE PEIDRA
EL GRAN CAMPEON
THE LOW WRITER............
ARTURO..................
BARCINAS...........................

Alcoholic, let me get an interview with you. What happened tonight? THIS SHITS FIXED! How am I gonna knock him down, bloody him up and lose his soul? I'll be back, he knows it. With the team I have in my corner, I'm sure we'll revise some kind of game plan to knock Arturo off his pedestal. Fuck that mutherfucker; don't worry, I have a re match clause. Let's do it again, tomorrow! Oh, here comes the Champ! The Alcoholic startled by the presence of Jesus and Arturo, flies out of the arena, yelling out; fuck you puto! I'll see you soon! Hahahahahahahahahaha! Arturo, sorry about that, he's a sore loser. Its ok, I'm used to it. I've been battling this fool for years now. On a higher note, I'd like to thank Jesus for guiding me in the right direction and supplying me with a great foundation and a beautiful game plan. This was by far, my greatest camp. I'd like to thank my familia and my church; I couldn't do it without your prayers. Last but not least, my mother ABI. This one's for you my love...

Arturo, what are you going to do after this sweet victory?

Get straight back to the drawing board, start writing again MVP MVP MVP MVP!

MIRROR

Mirror mirror on the wall
Why do they kick me when I'm down?

So you can get back up and write about it

FIRE

Arturo, you're playing with fire bro
I know, that's the story of my life
It's not the fire that concerns me
It's whether I burn from the consequences

THE PLAN

Sticking to his plan…
The hourglass running out of sand….
Mother Nature pissed; like we cheated on her…
The wicked on the rise; SURPRISE…..
As we scatter like roaches with our heads cut off
Judgment day around the block
Hoping we find the answers
Survey says; there are none…
This is his plan…
Coping, smoking dope
Evading White girl; losing hope
Venting my frustrations through my poetry…
Trying to be the best I can be as the world has the best of me…
Arturo's greatest hits…
Turning the other cheek
Slapped around by my own shadow; like a bald headed step child…
Hurdling over haters
Shot-putting the doubters
Running a relay race for my soul…
Looking back; as Satan tries to hand me the baton…
Fuck that…
It's all about my family….
Jesus rooting for me at the finish line
Art, just stick with my plan, you'll be fine…
The fat lady clearing her throat; trying to create a roadblock
Detours on every block; don't trust em

One hand on my bible; the other on my glock
Ain't no savior like the one I got….
Prayers all around the clock, 24/7
As the disbelievers and men with no faith finally understand……. all of a sudden
I ain't mad at cha; welcome to the team
Now let's get to work…
Working on an unleveled playing field
Picking poisonous fruit from the fields of self-destruction
Fishing for answers in the sea of corruption
Moby dick swallows my pride; I flick on my lighter, looking for the exit
Thinking to myself; maybe it's safer in here; as Satan tries to hand me the baton…
But I can't; have to stick to his plan
I'm telling you; I'm trying my hardest to stick to his plan…
Too scared to plan….
Hurricanes, war, massacres every single muthafucken day…
Too scared to have my kids go outside and play; real talk
Being played by our Government like a comedy; but this shits not funny…
Mingling with temptation
Flirting with redemption
Sleeping with the enemy
Married to God; I strive to be…
While my own people try to pry me off; like a snail on a wall…
Throwing me down with thunderous force; trying to crack my shell of faith…
But I'm hard boiled; blood boiling in a stew of tribulation
Breaking chains; hoping for change…
Chained up like a hungry rabid Doberman trapped on Kitty Cat Island…

Searching for salvation like a piece of hey in a needle stack…
That's where I'm at…
Prayer warrior working overtime……
Prayers for Florida
Prayers for Puerto Rico
Prayers for Mexico
Prayers for Vegas
Prayers for Korea
Prayers for Russia
Prayers for the Middle East…
Prayers for our soldiers…
Prayers for the families of the victims
Prayers for recovery
Prayers for the hungry
Prayers for the churches; one more time
Prayers for the churches…
Prayers for my people
Prayers for our people….
Thankful my family was out of harm's way; for today……..
If you're on the fence; now is as good a time as any
Fuck the life of flesh; I want to live forever
I just hope I can stick to his plan

WHITE GIRL

You had me at hello
Addiction at first night
I partied with you, OG and Mr. E
You were my favorite though
Lovers for three years
I still think about you
Still give in to you every once in a while
Every time I'm out, still look for you in the crowd
Knowing if I find you, you're mine
You introduced me to electronic music and parties on yachts
Kept me sober when I had too much
Made me a better lover
Beautiful memories that will last forever
TOO GOOD TO BE TRUE
That's why I had to leave
It wasn't till I left; I realized how much I loved you
I left because you took me out of reality

Till I see you again, White Girl
Thanks for taking a step back
I'm married with kids now

Love Art

MJ

My number one stunner
You've been with me for thirty years
Through my highest highs
And my lowest highs
Soothed my broken heart, time and time again
Always my sunshine when skies were grey
My anger management when I wanted fuck the world………..
Nourished my soul when had no appetite to live
Taught me patience and how not to judge others
Kept me cool and calm when times were distraught
Defused my insecurities and self-doubts
Helped bring out not only the lover, but the artist in me
You made me a better person
Thank you MJ for being a part of my journey called life
I appreciate you

Love Art

JUDGMENT DAY

Will the defendant please rise?

Yes my lord...

I; the King of Kings find you guilty of...
Lying, cheating, pride, jealousy, selfishness
drug and sex addiction.....
Uncountable counts of womanizing...
I also find you guilty of Love, Faith and
Humbleness

Before I read you your sentence, you have anything
to say for yourself?

Yes, I'm not sorry for my actions

Art Barcinas, in the name of the Father, Son and Holy Ghost
I sentence you to forgiveness and eternal life

Thank you

No, thank you for believing

ALL THE WAY

The score tied; 10 seconds left
4th and 25 on the 1 yard line
The gangsters of God with the ball in the I heart formation
The enemies in an illegal formation
It looks for a good time for a Hail Mary from Jesus....
RED 888, BLUE 888, OMAHA, GOD IS GOOD!
The snap!
Jesus hands the ball off to Arturo!
He finds a hole!
He shakes one enemy, and another!
HE
COULD
GO
ALL
THE
WAY!
He's at 50
The 40
The 30
Shakes another enemy as he high steps towards the end of
the world zone
The 10
The 5
TOUCHDOWN!
The crowd roars!
Oh, hold on, there's a flag on the play...
Holding, off sides and illegal use of the hands and mouth
Defense #666
Penalties declined, the gangsters win it!

MIRROR MIRROR

Mirror mirror on the wall
Why are you crying?

I'm shattered…
The world is fucked up

AFTER OUR FATHER

Our father prayer x1
I know I said it earlier; but I'll say it again
Thank you Lord for keeping me out of harm's way, for today

AMEN

WORDS FROM ABI

A few days after my Angel had passed, I stumbled upon
an archive of poems I had no idea existed. She had kept her
gift a secret all these years. Once I laid eyes on her words,
I immediately became inspired to become a writer. This is a
poem she wrote about me when I was a little boy. The more
I think about it, I truly believe her gift was passed on to me.
Thank you mama, I miss you……

MY SON

Of all the people in this world;
No one means more to me than you, my son.
You are my first born.
When I had you there was so much to learn.
Doctor said it's a boy!
The happiness and joy, you brought me a little boy.
You are indeed a boy.
With your messy room and all those toys.
Cards all over the place
When I want you to clean your room you give me a funny face.
You want to save them up you say
Because you want to become rich someday.
You are also very good in sports and in everything you do.
I am so proud of you.
You are also full of love,
But you are like a shy little dove.
My son, you will someday become a man.
There is nothing I can do about that,
But I will be there to understand.
Understand and be there Art,
When you first fall in love and even when someone breaks your heart.
You are my son and I will protect you anyway I can.
Be happy my son,
I will be proud of you whatever you choose to become.

THE END

ABOUT THE AUTHOR

Art Barcinas is a devoted Christian, husband and father of two. He enjoys sports, physical training, music and writing. His influences are his family, 2PAC, Sinatra, Al Green, Metallica and his alter egos, Art and Arturo. These are his stories about his life in his words; stories of addiction, heartbreak, adversity, redemption and LOVE.

Made in the USA
San Bernardino, CA
19 October 2017